The Tin Lodes

GW00482182

Andy Brown &
Marc Woodward

Indigo Dreams Publishing

First Edition: The Tin Lodes
First published in Great Britain in 2020 by:
Indigo Dreams Publishing
24, Forest Houses
Cookworthy Moor
Halwill
Beaworthy
Devon
EX21 5UU
www.indigodreams.co.uk

ISBN 978-1-912876-33-4

British Library Cataloguing in Publication Data. A CIP record for this book can be obtained from the British Library.

Designed and typeset in Palatino Linotype by Indigo Dreams.
Cover design from an original painting 'Woods above the River Teign, at Fingle Bridge' by James Tatum.
Copyright, James Tatum, SWAc _www.jamestatumartist.com_
With kind permission from James Tatum.
Printed and bound in Great Britain by 4edge Ltd.
Papers used by Indigo Dreams are recyclable products made from wood grown in sustainable forests following the guidance of the Forest Stewardship Council.

Andy Brown is Professor of English & Creative Writing at Exeter University and widely-known as a distinguished poet and writing tutor. His many poetry books include *Casket* (Shearsman, 2019); *Bloodlines* (Worple, 2018); *Watersong* (Shearsman, 2015); *Exurbia* (Worple, 2014); *The Fool and the Physician* (Salt 2012); *Goose Music* (with John Burnside, Salt 2008) and *Fall of the Rebel Angels: Poems 1996-2006* (Salt 2006), among others. He co-edited *A Body of Work: an anthology of poetry and medicine* (Bloomsbury, 2016) and edited *The Writing Occurs As Song: a Kelvin Corcoran reader* (Shearsman, 2015).

Marc Woodward's chapbook *A Fright of Jays* was published by Maquette Press in 2015 and his first full collection, *Hide Songs*, by Green Bottle Press in 2018. He has published poems in a wide variety of magazines, anthologies and websites and has performed his work regularly. He is also a highly respected musician and an internationally known mandolin player. Marc Woodward and Andy Brown perform live music together as *The SKPs*.

FOREWORD

The Tin Lodes is a collaboration in which each poem is anonymous. Although they were written by either one of us, each was written in response to the other's work. The poems were redrafted, edited and sequenced collaboratively. The intent is not for a guessing game as to who wrote which; only the collaboration matters.

We live on opposite sides of the river Teign in South Devon. To the west lies Dartmoor and the source of the river; to the east, lies the coast and the English Channel. The poems distill something of the natural, human and industrial history of these spaces. A few poems focus on specific historical figures, while others are inhabited by the anonymous generations who have lived and worked here on these ever-shifting rural and estuarine margins.

'The Tin Lodes' sequence itself stretches the catchment to the ruined tin mines on the nearby Cornish coast. The sequence centres on the Graeco-French character Pytheas of Massalia, the first trader to come to Britain and annex the mines for the Roman Empire. Several other poems explore the region's Roman heritage and its industrial history: tin, copper, granite and clay mining; fishing; agriculture, and other activities.

Extending the catchment further still, some poems reach across the world, with water as the circulating medium. Thinking about water like this led us to include myths associated with rivers, coasts and wells, as well as poems with overt ecological concerns. *The Tin Lodes* is therefore more than a regional project: it begins locally, but ends with an expansive idea of space in which trade and sea routes create ancient and modern coastlines... people connected to places; places connected to other places; times connected to times, and poet connected to poet and reader, through image and music, venture and adventure, creation and collaboration.

CONTENTS

The Tin Lodes

PULSE

I. Time

Picture a pendulum;
        the moon's patinated dial,
with each long sweep shifting

        the ocean back and forth,
scraping seashell dust along
        a mahogany floor.

II. Rhythm

Sea-tugged boats swing on their moorings,
rotating to a lunar beat.

Tethered to knotty trots regatta dinghies
founder and rise, levitating with the tide.

The ferry plies its trade across the harbour;
small queues grow and vanish on opposing shores.

Anglers arc bass lures overarm
then reel them back, tangled with weed.

Returning house martins feel another pull –
that of a slower, seasonal migration,

like the coach loads of summer tourists
who swell the bars in this seaside town

eating a cardiac of cod and chips,
banging empty pints on waspy tables.

Over the river the wealthy retired
shuttle from pharmacy to village shop,

until blue lights block the street,
while a doctor gently seeks a pulse.

III. Repeat

A sea so calm it holds the stars
    in yellow stains. And nearer,

on the cooling sand two starfish
    in a lovers' kiss, left by the change.

The new tide unclutters the beach.
    Morning sweeps the stars from the sea.

These planes and mirrors circle and repeat.
    The grit of stars and shells grinds at our feet.

A SPRINKLING

The River Teign, from the Anglo Saxon Teng, 'a stream'.
Related to the pre-Roman Welsh Taen: 'a sprinkling'.

I.

A stream,
  a sprinkling,
    from separate sources...
a Birder lifts his lenses for a hawk and sees
a Neolithic woman at Teign Head, beating
her fists on her chest as she buries her dead.
The body lies beneath a moorland cairn,
but the risen water transports the soul
under the clapper bridge at Teigncombe.

Nearby at Grey Wethers, a cider-soaked farmer
mistakes the circled stones for sheep
and freshens up his face in the riffles
of the joining southern stream. From a corrie,
through loose schist left by prospectors,
the flume plunges down an inclined clough
to where the mountain avens grow and shed
their burrs on the fur of indifferent dogs
as they run through the stone huts and reaves
abandoned now to wind and the merging cries
of Vikings and monks at the burning Abbey.

Along the levels past Teignharvey and Teignmouth,
trains speed inland to the moor, their passengers
gazing on the river through their own reflections,
at mussel pickers boot-high in alluvium,
at flounder fishermen beside their tripods –
the rods of their hopes leant *toward heaven still*,
their baited lines weighted and waiting. A child
points out a harbour seal with mermaid eyes
hunting for mackerel and bass between the boats.

The train runs through a sprinkling of towns
with their manoral halls where scribes sign off
the deeds of the Great Court of Tinners,
the peat-cutting contracts and records
of villages overcome by Black Death,
their bridges crossed by fleeing villagers –

the wooden bridge that once conveyed
Norman footmen; the red stone bridge
across the Domesday salt marsh;
the pristine white stone of the Roman walkway;
the 70s viaduct with her eleven spans;
the Victorians crossing at Shaldon
in boaters, parasols and Sunday best.

At the confluence with Walla Brook,
flowing from Hangingstone Hill,
a man crawls through the Tolmen Stone
to cure his rheumatism; his arthritis;
chafing off disease on the stone's rough skin.
A child was passed through here. Another
through hooped brambles. And one more still
through a hole in the ground. Reborn.

The Birder shifts his viewfinder to watch
two farmers shaking hands through the ring,
to seal a binding deal on tups and wethers.
Beside a waymarker, a pilgrim cups his hands
and stares back at the Birder through its void
to gain second sight, a future beheld, a glimpse
of heaven on the way through Fernworthy.

He leaves the moor along the Hunters' Path
past Bovey and her ball-clay works, the ghost
of the old power station puffing into the air,
as her turbines cool down in the current,
out to the estuary, the tidal Whitelake Channel
and her kaolinitic canals, concreted over now
for a retail park near the weekend racecourse.

II.
The sun's high arc warms up the mingling tides.

Light vapours rise around the anchored yachts –
a longing that seems to climb from the creek,

up around the pillars of the bridge
that cinctures the waist of the river
at the cusp between inlet and marshland,

where warblers chitter in the willow carr
and spark the air like the chattering voices
of hedgers and osier cutters who twist
withies and pleaches beside their bothy.

Out on the saltings, where the inlet's mud
breaks-up like the cracks on a canvas,
a conclave of waders watch a Bronze Age
fisherman navigate his coracle

over to a niche in the rocks. He chants
his hunting prayer and parts a veil
of seaweed to reveal cormorant squabs

awaiting a parent and fish for their gullets.
Downstream the overflow pipe lets slip

its secret, jarring song into the sea.

FLOW
i.m. Dr Rose Polge

I.

Persistent waves come shipping their cargo:
plastic bottles scrubbed clean of their labels,
hanks of rope, branches and boxes which hang
on the underside of bullying foam,
their buoyancy almost giving up its ghost.

The sea curates the dead. Spring tides wash up
torn boughs, anonymous bones, ammonites.
The dual planes of the tide, in and out,
up and down, suggest it stays close. *Your* sea,
rotating detritus from *your* river.

It's not like that. The sea flows slowly east,
a cortège for flotsam and surrender...
In seven weeks a lost doctor traversed
Lyme Bay from Anstey's Cove to Portland Bill.

II.

Today for hours along the shored-up front
two blokes from the Environment Agency
have mapped a slick of swelling, emerald dye
they've tipped into the sea between the groynes.

They're trying to measure how, and when, the waves
traverse the beach; how long it takes for tides
to wash away what people have constructed –

the stress and strain on pier and harbour wall –
how wind and choppiness affect the slick,
these valencies and energies that might
upset the soft geometry of beaches.

Beyond their heads, and those of lounging bathers;
beyond the sails of yachts and cargo ships,
the doctor's body drifts on unmarked waves.

MY LAST SEASCAPE

Thomas Luny, maritime painter, lived in Teignmouth.

'Neptune taming a sea-horse.'
   ~ *'My Last Duchess'*, **Robert Browning**

Here's my last seascape hanging on the wall.
See how it brings the shifts in light and shade
up to the fore in tricks of textured pigment;
the ever-changing aspects of the sea,
the marbled sky, the knots and swags of rigging.
I finished it from memory in my room.

My male attendant used to wheel me out
to take the air in my perambulator
down to the Den, or over to the Point
where the Teign joins the sea in crossed currents,
and there would station me at my easel,
set up my cabinet of colours, brushes
and watch me start to fashion the rough shapes
on canvases for merchants and sailors –
the Viscount of Exmouth; Admiral Tobin;
Old John Spratt; Captain Brine and Captain Wight.
I'd sell them back their own heroic deeds,
'The Battle of the Nile', 'The Bombardment
of Algiers', or a soft sketch of a storm,
the river Teign and Shaldon by the Ness
with vessels coming in and out of harbour,
the Parson and the Clerk by Dawlish cliffs,
pack horses bringing red rocks in for building...

But what's the point in painting summer scenes
sparkling with pleasure boats and packed ferries;
what point, when the melancholy ocean
presents itself: a gale, a hurricane,
the stricken *Madelina* drifting ashore,
her bowsprit and her masts destroyed, her crew

all five-hundred perished? I have known
the indifferent sea, the behaviour
of ships in every form of wind and weather,
the place and use of every cleat and rope;
the friction of those ropes against my skin.
And what hands are these that can no longer hold
a brush? My fingers bent in on my palms,
clutching the paint-laden thing at arm's length
between these useless fists. Dabbing. Dabbing.
What will they say of me? Will they say
that he was fair and florid? Of medium build?
That he was taciturn but kind? An elderly invalid
with paralysed legs and a naval pension?

I have signed and dated my last seascape
there on a block of floating wood, a spar.
See how it drifts. I've spent my best days here.
Now lay me down to rest in Devon soil.

ROCKS AND FISH

'We know who we are. We are who we are
the day we are born, spend the rest of our lives
becoming someone else, like rocks in rising tides.'
       ~ *'Cavatina', **Andy Brown***

becoming someone else, like rocks in rising tides
you say, but I wonder if the opposite's true:
that actually we emerge from swilling waters,
the ocean receding to leave us bare, exposed
to weathering. The sun and ice, bake and shatter.

Mine is a more obvious metaphor of course
and on reflection I think yours more accurate.
Are we ever more perfect than when we are young –
newly cleaved, salt washed and as yet barnacle free?
What follows then is gradual dissolution in
the hydrosphere of energy and nothingness.

Steam swirls and condenses as I lie in the bath
shaving with my right hand, while my Parkinson's left
flaps mindlessly – like a fish urgent for the sea.

BEACH HUTS

April means unlocking, sweeping off spiders
and sand, putting out to air the rug,
stripy beach towels and faded sun-loungers.
Checking the kettle, rinsing out the mugs.
Shutting the fridge for beer and lemonade.
Washing down the body board, bucket, spade.

When they opened *Springtide* they found Alice,
still as a waxwork in a garden chair,
dry as blown sand, her dress nibbled by mice.
They'd never thought to look for her in there.
Police believed she'd gone to Birmingham,
judging from some grainy CCTV –
back where her own spring tide once ran.
Her rigid fist was locked around the key.

CALF EYE

The clump of gawkers stood around to watch
a digger lift the dead calf from the beach.

A Devon red, its beaten hide sand-caked,
twisted legs flung out, lying like it might
have dug its way up from a darker place
to die satisfied in ozone and light.

The driver heel-screwed his cigarette,
climbed in the cab and turned toward the calf.

Its clouded eye stared up, blindly pointing
at the canvas sky. A polished pebble,

quartz and slate embedded in a slab
of sand and hair. An eye that once looked

through a thin fence without understanding.
The digger chuntered in. We turned aside.

FLOOD

The levee broke and the flatlands flooded
up to the farmhouse door. A cow swam by
and all manner of stuff floated round.

For six green months she'd sat in her room,
looked out across the constant meadows,
watched cattle come and go, taking their turn,
saw seagulls stamping turf to summon worms.

The rooks grew feather trousers, balding beaks,
while slowly the levee was springing leaks,
bulging for a thunderstorm to snap.

For all that time her mind was parched
and to slake some kind of thirst she lay
down in a deluge of poor-boy music.
Stolen blues and songs of desolation.

Now the levee had burst she might move on.
When the water drained. She was just dry,
Hardtack dry. In need of rehydration.

TIDELAND

At low tide
a wide sandbank
rises in the river.
A flat Salty
where gulls mine
for lugworms
and the oystercatchers' skirl
sails the water.
On cockle-bucket days
we canoe to this island
beach our boats and stay
on the wave-slapped sand
until the new tide washes us away.
When the ayot breaches
on black-glass nights
it cracks the moon's mirror
into stippled lace.
Lost and reclaimed,
midnight to noon,
this sea-given land,
this land in the call of the moon.

GLASS EELS

The yawning, limitless sea
awash with tides of plankton

wakes up with the magnetised
muscles of eels as they migrate

across the delta's fan, the endless
sands of untouched beaches,

up the brackish stretch and into
fresh headwaters, oncoming streams,

where clutching frogs lay spawn
in moorland pools; where heather

multiplies its bells for bees,
dropping their florets for woodlouse and worm;

where two Adonis blue butterflies lap
at a lump of fox scat lying on a rock...

and on they push, these elvers, on and on
upstream, until they reach the tarn

among the tors and rocks, each boulder
made from untold spiral shells,

from countless compressed plankton rising
up from the deep, the bottomless past.

EEL CATCHING

A midnight fog lays down the land,
sucks quietly on the ploughed field,
wetly kisses the upturned sod.
Whispers from the river mouth
the fetid smell of marsh decay.
The moon and stars, obscured by mist
stare upon other worlds tonight.
Time passes with no sense of motion.
The Earth lies still – except for me,
by the river, waiting for eels.

Now, into this brackish reach the tide is running.
Sliding through underwater grass,
current tracers in the blind depth,
I can sense them – the eels are coming…
The small bell on the rod end rings,
I strike and take a fat one on:
shiny with slime, a liquid figure of eight.
I haul it to the bank, blackest in the blackness,
thrashing fiercely in the torchlight,
as if in tongues before the priest.

Later, as I walk through the wet grass
knee high by the silent river,
the eel still twists in the plastic bag
flapping briskly at my side.
On the back door step I do the act.
So much dark blood, like thick red oil,
flowing out toward the ground.
Still the eel moves in defiance,
blood without and blood within,
this deathless, lifeless, other thing.

THE SYZYGY LINE

A confluence of forces:
Sun, Moon, Earth, Water.

Slow beach Sundays spent
lying in the paper arms
of hot afternoons.

Birders on the Teign,
tea-cupped in their hide, take bets.
Terns and avocets.

River mist mornings
haunted by little egrets;
undertaker coots.

The Teign in flood bears
unwanted gifts from the moor.
Dead sheep tied with twigs.

This year was so dry
that when the spring tide went out
we found stone footprints.

The bright sun has rude
intentions on the shaved heads
of hatless young men.

Gull mobs are hustling
their defecation racket
on the street outside.

Palm roots are shrugging
off pavement slabs by the Den
all over again.

SEA PRIMER

1. Matins / **Midnight** / *Eight Bells*
The ocean is a Book of Hours
inscribed in light's calligraphy.
The stylus is the gannet's bill
emblazoning the sea.

2. Lauds / **3 a.m.** / *Six Bells*
You wake before me, quietly rise,
your eyes still puffed with sleep.
This morning rite's a trawling line
that hauls me from the deep.

3. Prime / **6 a.m.** / *Four Bells*
Beneath an upturned arch of tile
the crab collector probes his finger.
Two hundred baited traps to check
where crab and crayfish linger.

4. Terce / **9 a.m.** / *Two Bells*
The mussel beds now lie exposed,
the mussel men pull on their kit.
The mussels pull their blue shells closed
and the hungry seabirds wait.

5. Sext / **Midday** / *Eight Bells*
The captains of the fishing boats
unload their catch from stinking hulls.
They clean the fish and chuck the guts
to the gluttony of gulls.

6. *None* / **3 p.m.** / *Two Bells*
The river pilot guides a ship
around the point and into port,
while kayakers and pleasure craft
head out to sea in search of sport.

7. *Vespers* / **6 p.m.** / *Four Bells*
The oystermen have cleared their racks,
on shore the pubs have lit their lamps.
In restaurants along the front
broad oyster knives work at the clamps.

8. *Compline* / **9 p.m.** / *Two Bells*
The Russian tanker docked at bay
sits weighted to the Plimsoll line.
Like herons picking sprats from shoals
the derricks empty her by nine.

OYSTER SHELLS

'He was a bold man that first ate an oyster.'
                    ~ Jonathan Swift

Neptune's castanets
clacking an apt sea shanty.
Stones with a mind of their own.
Tears of some bouldered Colossus
littering the tidal causeway.
Crocks for a prized aphrodisiac.
The heart prised apart.
The Fort Knox of pearls.
Rough tokens in an ancient trader's hands.
Skin scissors – the bane of bare feet.
Social climbers, from Cheapside to the Ritz.
Rockerfellers of the strand.
Saviours of weak bones
and dreamers of New World homes
built from Tabby concrete.

Cups of salty liquor.
          Shore squatters.
                    The Devil's toenails.

LITHOLOGIES / MYTHOLOGIES

Written to celebrate the bicentenary of William Smith's first geological map of Britain.

He steps today from West to East
journeying through space and time,

from Mesozoic Dorset's Scroff
and Forest Marble, its Zigzag Bed,

all the way to Cretaceous Kent's
Gault Clay, Greensand and Chalk.

As he walks across the southern Downs,
the shallow, warm Jurassic seas

unveil the blueprint for a map –
a portrait of the country and the man –

Strata Smith, canal engineer, testing
the Somerset coal seams, the Slyving

and the Dungy Drift, the Perrink,
the Rudge above the Temple Cloud,

the Nine Inch and the Coking Coal.
Strata Smith, the drainage man,

who turns those boggy yards of mud
to workable farms; rinsing his Pundibs

and Pound-Stones, to show how fossils are
a haunting from the underlying past

and write their certain history on the land,
burying old myths of Flood and Creation.

Today, at the foot of the Society's stairs
the curtains part, unveiling the map.

Its colours shine where science meets art:
the green for Chalk, the purple Coral Rag,

Prussian Blue Lias, Grey wash for the Clunch,
the honey of his treasured Oolites.

FISH AND STONE

Granite once flowed from this river.
Hewn from the high moorland quarries
then shipped to rebuild London Bridge.

Those quarries now are brambled pools,
though chiselled rock still hunkers there,
brooding in its flooded prison.

After weeks at sea the doggers
of the Newfoundland fisheries
landed their salted catches here

until the cod were overfished
and the scattered shoals sent boats home
with empty holds to hungry docks.

Now white kaolinitic clay
graded from the Bovey basin
fills the dockside sheds and coasters.

Mica chips from forty million
years of granite degradation
brighten porcelain and toothpaste.

In trade: fertiliser arrives,
made from the ground bones of livestock,
bones white as ball clay or cod flesh.

The wharf side cranes swing out and reach.
Fish, clay, feed and bone. Their huge weight
dainty on a thousand years of stone.

THE OLD BOATYARD

He measured out the working day in tea breaks,
his rambling dock piled high with tools and motors;
a flock of anchors stacked against the wall;
jerry cans of two-stroke, engine oil;

discarded prop-shafts, boss caps and, to one side,
rusting under tarps beneath the windows,
their panes obscured by webs and smuts of grease...
the deconstructed heart of some old cruiser.

Work could always wait until the tea
had brewed – the biscuits dunked – then he would dig
his boots and spanner out and disappear
inside a hull, to jump start the machine.

Now there's a prefab; a steel & glass cabin.
Some new bloke with a clipboard and a rota.

THE KILNERS

Two men ignited the bones of the past
one Monday, late in the year's dark corner.

Boats weighed anchor off the Ness on Tuesday,
awaiting high tide and a hold of lime.

By Wednesday combustion was well progressed,
with a caustic stench and skin-peeling heat.

In Thursday's moonlight the smoke ascended
like the twisted spire of Ermington church.

On Friday the pall-bearer night wore no gloves;
shattering wherever it laid its pale hand –

only the blistering lime kiln was spared
and the two men who slept close to its wall

flanking their deadly charge. During the night
the young burner rolled into the fire.

Whether the boy was choked by toxic smoke
or wooed the heat too closely none could say,

but he burned with insufficient fuss
to rouse the slumbering quarryman.

Saturday the kiln was cooling, ticking down
to Sunday when his riddlings could be raked.

IGNITION

A squall from nowhere chased us off the beach
to a ruined lime kiln's musty shelter.
Mossy walls curved up to an open mouth
which once vented sparks. A natural skylight –
Pantheonesque with the rain tumbling in.

At least we are out of the wind, you said,
your wet hair beach-tangled, your chest rising.
You lifted your face to the ring of light
and the diamond raindrops showering down.
Your siren's throat sang out to be kissed.

A jade necklace of foliage clambered
down the brickwork. I leaned in to your heat
and that moment of ignition moved us
through quick and slaked – to smoke flailing in wind.

SONG OF A LENGTHMAN

Beyond that brilliant hank of orange twine
laid down here by the bloke whose piebald calves
lick at the bitter salt-block in the meadow…

beyond the rotting fence post where the thrush,
mottled like a log, flits from the twisted wire
that cuts beneath the beech tree's silvered bark
above the tawny cushion of its leaf fall…

and, down, beyond the crimson bolts of dock
and maple stems budding by the rusted
knifeblade of the river…   here, today,

two black-caps forage near the turning eye
of a slow-stirred pool, their dun-brown fledgling
nestled on a trunk, coaxing him to take off,
up, and further up, into the startling blue.

TOLL ROAD

Coach and horses ~ 1 Shilling
One score of oxen or cattle ~ 10d

You take the withered road,
once high and boastful
before the broom of bypass
swept it to a ramble.
Ragwort claims the verges;
dunnocks fill the hedges.

One horse or beast drawing any
cart ~ coach ~ waggon ~ landau ~ 6d

You take the withered road
beside a spectral pony.
The shadow route –
running half-heartedly
under flapping leaves
of whistlewood trees.

Bullock ~ 2d

You take the withered road,
crooked as a crone's mouth,
to read the toll boards
on hexagonal houses
by granite bridges
at village edges.

Every horse laden or unladen ~ 1 1/2d
Pedestrian ~ 1d

Enough for a weathered traveller
walking in cracked boots
from one congregation –
to find the same removed;
perhaps tinkering saucepans?
Seeking a barton needing hands?

No tinkers

A man who doesn't choose
the poacher's path through trees;
who doesn't slink in the meadows
to swing by a branch upstream.
You take the withered road
prepared to pay the toll.

Church and funeral traffic ~ exempt

THE TIN LODES

'Phlebas the Phoenician, a fortnight dead,
Forgot the cry of gulls, and the deep sea swell
And the profit and loss.'
~ *'Death by Water', The Waste Land,* **T.S. Eliot**

'this foundry for sounds' ~ *Dart,* **Alice Oswald**

I. Kestrel at Geevor

The *kee-kee* of a hunting Windhover
chimed through the spires of the tin mine chimneys.

It stooped from one element to another,
from floating point of fantailed stasis
down into the thatch of grass and thrift,

dropping like a stream of molten metal
from crucible to mould; striking its prey
and shipping it by talon to a post
where the bronzed beak was dipped, the bones picked clean.

Beyond, the one-eyed stannary chimneys
watched the kill with ancient disregard –
weathered coastal sentries in spring sunshine
that could have been the ruins of Mycenae,
or Herodotus's *Cassiterides*.

II. Pytheas of Massalia
3rd century BC, Marseilles

Pytheas of Massalia, steps from his barque,
orders his oarsmen to anchor, be silent,
out of the reach and the roil of the surf
that breaks beyond the turmoiled turquoise world.
His carious teeth glint in the Cornish sun.
(*The Romans are coming. The Romans!*)
His legion rows ashore and seals the site.

Anatolian slaves from the Empire quake
in this forsaken, windswept backwater,
burning with knowledge of copper, tin, bronze
and an era's cutting edge weaponry.

Beneath his sandaled feet, Pytheas sees
the cuprous stripes that bleed across the rocks.
'Our hands will soon control the trading route…'

III. Buddling

To Geevor then we came
heading West to East
along the sandy road
above the spent tin lodes.

Walking beside you, Kelvin,
a kestrel high in the air
(and a geek's remote-control drone),
we were buddling for nuggets

in talk of the shadowy past,
smelting the impure ore of memory
into the white metal of *Now*
in a place that resonates with far away.

Some epiphanies, you said,
we can surely live without.

IV. The Trade Routes

Mr Pytheas, the Marseilles merchant
can still hear the cicadas of the Med
in the cries of these gulls a thousand miles
from home. He'll want to keep the source a secret
from those get-rich-quick traders he has left
behind – the mob of Marseilles millionaires.

'They'll get their tin from Ictis soon enough,
carted back across the channel, down the Rhône
to Gaul.   I, Pytheas, minter of tin,
entrepreneur, am resistant to corrosion;
to their ruin and corruption. Consider
what they will do with the money I bring.
Get themselves some teeth! Some morals!'

V. The Coffin Works

What happened to Piran?
He's gone under ground –
thirty-one men at pick and shovel
buried alive and drowned.

Treeve and Santo, Rewan and Pascow.
Benesek and Branoc, Arthek and Clemo.
Our founder, the sea-lord, old Meryasek,
Costentyn, no longer firm. And bold Hedrek.

Their bodies are undone. Their names live only.
They haunt the shafts and adits
while their wives and Bal Maidens –
those Ladies of the Rocks – are lonely.

Their tallow candles long blown out.
Their long home in the wind's redoubt.

VI. The Devil's Metal

Pytheas, mineral lord of Massalia,
oversees the stamp and crazing mill;
pays tribute to his captains underground.

Blasting the stopes out with black powder
Thomas Epsley blew himself yonder in 1689.
John Archer at Trebollans mine
followed him in '91 'while shuting rocks'.

The beelemen advance the drift,
chip away the ore and deads
and, where the lode dips slopewise,
the shovelmen barrow it back

bringing the broad scoop to bear,
up to the shambles and into the light
by hoisters with a pair of balanced keebles.

VII. Material Men

Pytheas and his Anatolians
unearth the copper zones beneath the tin.

Their water wheels and pumps exhaust the leat.
Above them, kestrels hover for fresh meat.

What do you want it for, Adventurer, Tutworker;
wherefore this silver-white stannum?

For bronze. For solder. Tins of peas.
A tube of paste to shine your teeth.

The windward escarpment sings 'Profit & Loss'
to these material men. Over the peaks

of the already ancient boulders
the arid plains of the Med are calling home.

'But all *that* is behind me,' cries Pytheas.
'All *that* is nothing but a deep sea swell.'

VIII. Coda

The plunging winzes scored into the surface
were fenced off for the care of visitors.
The shafts and level mining of the cliff works
outlined the branded fields of heritage.

We stopped beside a ventilation shaft,
our girls gone on ahead of us, rounding
the bluff. The kestrel still *kee-kee*'d above,

or was that the rhythm of poll picks,
plugs and feathers, chisels,
splitting the rocks down below?

Out in the bay a tall ship rounded
the point, tailed by a fleet of Phoenicians.
At our feet, the weathered outcrops
glinted underneath the oil and tar.

RISE AND FALL

I. Zephyrus

I am Westerly,
chasing over cliffs and moors.
I do as I please.

The sculptor of trees,
architect of rocky tors.
All answer to me.

I raise the cold seas
and dash them into the land.
I do as I please.

The farmer throws seeds
broadcasting with his right hand.
All answer to me.

Boatmen bless the breeze
for a haul of cod and ling.
I do as I please.

Phoenician galleys
blew here for rich seams of tin.
All answer to me.
I do as I please.

II. Dagan

'Who has not seen the scarus rise,
decoyed and killed by fraudulent flies?'
> *~ **Marcus Valerius Martialis**, Roman poet, fisherman and source*
> *of this first description of fly fishing.*

Where the Teign descends from withy moorland,
quick under sloe and red-berried rowan,
scrapes over grit into fly-whirling pools
where slivers of brownies waggle and flit –

Martial the poet took twelve foot of silk,
a Hare's Ear nymph tied with feathers from Rome;
and with a neat flick put a hook in the lip
of the fish god Dagan – Dew of the Land –

a Merman in azure and olive scales
burnished as bright as a Lazio noon,
crowned with cassiterite, cloaked in the moon.

Swiftly unhanded he slipped the God back
to the hollow water. Cold western winds
sucked up the sea into chough-feather clouds.

III. Ceres

Mothering the native earthworms,
she runs new soil through ancient hands
to gauge its mineralogy.
Her spelt bends in the wind between
the tinners' moor and Romans' sea.

When late spring pulses through the woods
and vivid sprigs of Bread-and-Cheese
squeeze out the early blackthorn bloom,
she flows across the ground to spread
her tendrils, seeds, mycelium.

Under stony burial mounds
where the redundant are interred
she brings her family of worms.
By her ministry nothing dies
but only rots to be reborn.

In this cold clutch of Devon soil
the remnants of her followers
who tilled the dirt – a reaper band –
lie with the Three Hares' mining men
who tin-panned Dartmoor's smelting land.

IV. Whitehorse Hill

Hard through the cotton grass and boulders
she came up Whitehorse Hill to find you –
a 'high ranking female' in a moorland cist –
she, a shaman of tools and trapped lightning.

Four thousand silent years of separation
led to this singular co-incidence,
the peat hag collapsing: your tomb open
for a trowel-poking archaeologist.

She tweezers through your ashes, picks apart
your embers, pulls aside your winding sheet
(cloth: nettle-fibre); inspects your bracelet
(neatly woven cow hair, tarnished tin plate);

rolls your collection of precious trinkets
between her university fingers
(smooth spooled ear studs turned from spindle wood,
consistent with the local flora).

In your lime-bark basket nestle amber beads
from Baltic woods beyond a skylark's sight.
Who would travel such a way to find you?
She turns the beads, imagines wearing them.

V. Roman Roads

I strip the chestnut leaves to fish bones
as a squall pounds the dark canopy.

Freshly washed, the fat river freights the rain
to meet the tide and inundate the port.

Over the estuary the martial drum
of a Paddington train warps on the wind.

Weeks back I'd driven home on the Fosse Way,
direct as a centurion's sword.

Roof down, chariot style, through the soft wolds,
Moreton, Stow, Corinium; recalling

how Romans imported the chestnut trees,
their saplings erect by villas and camps.

After the empire packed-up its galleys,
cloven shells littered these roads and ditches.

Today Canada geese divide the clouds
honking westwards in triumphal Vs.

They too were once migratory, tracking
magnetic senses through metallic skies.

Now they're residents and those high routes
have blown loose – the way forgotten roads

give in to nettles, grass and fallen husks.

TWO WATER NYMPHS

I. Coventina
Queen of the Celtic river goddesses

She walked beside the estuary in search
of the last of her kind. *Who is this?*
asked the world and, though we cannot know

exactly what it was the birds observed,
the godwits sang of darkness and the terns
of skittered fish that skimmed across the surf.

The trees that lined the riverbank supposed
that she was wandering far from home
on the wind's uprooted breath.

A smirr of mist described her as a secret
ocean; a yearning reservoir; a desert
quenched by unrelenting rain.

The moon's dry hum was of her restlessness,
while the stars replied that she was pure
mathematics, the realness of reality.

Mostly she is mud, sang earth,
and what's not mud is water.
Only the river knew she was a shift

in the way things flowed; a book
of teeth and bones that, centuries from now,
might come to light beneath her timeless bed.

II. Arnemetia

Romano-Celtic water goddess. Those who
drank from her well were cured of sickness.

Every time she pulled a wishbone
this was what she asked for:

that the dead, each year, be woken up
and welcomed back to join her;

that they should come and celebrate
with dance and song, with drink and fire

and, every time she lit a fire, she wished
that she might scale tomorrow's tower

and up there on the summit run
her fingers down the Milky Way's bright spine.

Each time she saw a shooting star she wished
that she might always be so grounded,

to come into the garden through leaf-fall
and log-rot, through fruit-burst

and the sweet corruption of mushrooms
budding by her well, their gaze raised skyward.

SOME SAYINGS ABOUT THE CORMORANT

The lone black huntress
senses the presence of prey,
dives and liquefies.

In the space she leaves
what can be said of the world?
She's her own absence.

She resurfaces,
one eye in the Cretaceous,
the other in myth.

Owning the channel
she extends her wings to dry –
a hook-faced Harpy.

The cormorant fills
her wattles; rattles her song –
this raucous Siren.

Compelled by the tide
and the pull of shoaling fish,
we scull through her wake.

HERONS

Grey as the watery dawn,
wet with the guts of frogs,
the blood of moorhen chicks,

Ardea cineriae:
ghosts upon the foreshore,
patient for fish and history.

Separate and sentinel,
misplaced milestones, attendants
to the helicoidal flow

which undermines the river bank
(the sliding snake that slowly
eats the water-meadow).

Their perfumed legs
are nectar to minnows
who crowd to be speared;

their beaks – the impalers
of stooping falcons.
Crepuscular anglers,

these willowy hernshaws
come and watch and go
like cousins of the moon,

delicate and granite,
timid but constant,
observers and recorders.

Beneath their plumage
their hollow bones
are etched with runes:

the unreadable toll
of the seasons' cycles,
the pool of the river.

EQUINOX

I. Autumn

Axle end moon,
sitting justly
on a flat horizon.

Inverted fulcrum:
the balance point
of dark and light.

The seesaw tips,
we cross the meridian
into the long shake
of hibernation nights,

the drop of logs in hearths,
the fug of damp coats hanging
in mouldering hallways
of winter hearts.

II. Vernal

A sideways slip of balance brings us,
almost un-noticing,
into this new atmosphere.

Lorries on the motorway
hum drone-songs through skinny air.
I'm sure they're moving faster,
urgent now to be somewhere.

Driving home in defected daylight
past budding trees on Spinney Lane:
the uncurling spring is here.

TRIBUTARIES

I. Templer Way Abecedary

Arch Brook, Bundle Head,
Clay Works, Drum Bridge.

Esplanade, Five Wyches,
Gabwell, Hunters Lodge.

Ilford Park, Jetty Marsh,
Kiln Brake, Lower Down.

Mortimer's Farm, No Man's Land,
Old Quay, The Point.

Quarry Road, Rope Walk,
Sewage Works, Tracey House.

Ullacombe, Ventiford,
Wildwoods Point, Forches Cross.

Set out on foot from Yarner Wood.
Arrive downstream at Shaldon Zoo.

II. The Dark Acre

The cleves above the oggin glower
in the dimmet evening, as if cursed
by the Dewer himself.   Dinder
rolls across the tors. The sky is owdry.

By morning an ammil of ice will glaze
the leaves that hang across the taw
this spring melt. Soon, perhaps,
the tawds will leave toddies in puddles.

Along the holloway a brock
disappears through the unket shord
where the craw at the wind-bent kone
taunts the mommet scaring birds;

where the past's lie-a-biers are mired
in clobb, in clats of earth, on this dark acre.

III. Pubs and Moorings

By these inns the river flows:
Warren, Stag and Tally Ho!
Pumped down from the heady moors
Teign House, Rock Inn, Old Black Horse,
through the woods and lowland farms
Ploughman's Rest, Claycutter's Arms,
widening to meet the sea,
Jolly Sailor, Jolly Brise.

Here is where we sleep the boats:
some pulled up and some afloat
by the fish quay's twisted nets,
Silver Spit and Polly Steps.
Near the stack of lobster pots
Butterbanks and Crownwell trots.
Nothing will be free here soon,
half trot, whole trot, or pontoon.

MILLIONAIRES' ROW

Along the waterline a daybreak fox
scavenges through tidal remnants.
Chinoiserie egrets alight and wait.
It's a black-stump dawn for cormorants.

With wings outstretched, a new divorcee
mimes tai chi on her waterfront lawn.
Her husband bunked off with a sailor –
now she's marooned in a fogbound home.

She's looking to sell her boathouse off,
declaring she's *moored to the riverside*.
The villagers snort *it's a London sum*.
The birds materialise with each low tide,

unruffled by escalating prices
or how fishing shacks have been removed,
replaced by architectural fancies:
hardwood decks, patient hot tubs, sedum roofs.

Slack water reveals the dark skeleton
of weed-hung pilings where mussel chains
were once the locals' livelihood. Wings wide,
black cormorants surrender to the change.

THE GREEN SHALL INHERIT

Put the sky behind you and clamber down
from the wind-harried ridge to the deep coombe.

The air becomes still, the trees exhausting.
June the third and these plants would consume you

if such was their nature. Turn and turn back:
the weeds sprout even while you look away.

Drop to the bridle track, shrink to the beads
of dew, cuckoo spit froth, blackberry spike,

stick, splinter and mould. Ant, aphid, woodlouse,
and all the catastrophic underworld

are attending to their chores: chopping up
flags of leaves; new buds bulging in their spoil.

Careless, instinctual, organic – they're all
just a plague away from taking over.

Now shrink smaller still, down to the crazy
ommatidia of a beetle's eye,

look through a foliage kaleidoscope –
observatory to a mushroom sky.

BEACH TROVE

Needle skeletons of mercury bones –
the wind's own death-rattle marimba.
A grinning garfish, stinking and flyblown.

Hypodermics; tampons; prophylactics.
The detritus of sex, drugs and gender.
A shingle of abalone plastic.

Messages in bottles, each one the same.
Enough rope to hang the Earth from its pole.
Timber: twisted limbs, broken pallet frames.

Torn from a mooring a tyre with no tread;
an old Nike trainer missing its sole.
A beached whale. A doll's head. All of it dead.

BOWMAN'S LAMENT

When I let fly and heard the bowstring thwack
against the yew and saw the arrow loose –
I knew. Just knew. The sky stepped sideways,
shivered at the brush of fletching as the shaft
flew past and rushed on up to the white moon.
Her lonely face punctured and deflated,
skeltered down into the confused sea
swilling on the beaches in uncertainty.

I was cursed by owls, foxes, moths, voles.
All those nocturnal acolytes of moonlight:
astronauts, dancers, lovers. Poets too.
Me? I'm the man who shot down the moon,
who becalmed the turbulent oceans;
who brought the blue green earth to ruin.

THE SURFER KING

This is my last request of those I love:
I'm wiped out now – carry me to the cove,
not on my surfboard, but a wicker chair,
then point me at the sea and leave me there.

I'll sit and count each fabled seventh wave
then gather beach glass washed from mermaids' graves
with which I'll open up my arteries
and let my weary blood flow to the sea.

Poseidon falling from Atlantic highs
come take my heart for a halibut's eye.
Let my rib cage form a sieve of baleen
to skim all plastic, leave the oceans clean.

Take my demented brain for isinglass.
Repurpose me. This is my wish. My last.

ETERNAL RETURN

My mother gave my father's body back
inside a plastic bottle filled with grit.

I scattered it from boulders on Hay Tor
where they had honeymooned in sixty one.

She took her husband's ashes on the plane
and flew them to a beach just north of Perth –

a landmark in the story of themselves
where she entrusted them to southern seas.

Standing on the shoreline by the harbour,
deep currents mingle at the river's mouth...

I'm waiting for the elements to bring
my father's wandering body back together:

a fleck of heart on cold winds from the hills,
a mote of bone on currents from the south.

LONG PASSAGE

'I love …
The places where water comes together
With other water.'
>   ~ **Raymond Carver**

The herons of Netherton Woods
are standing still to watch the stillness
that hangs at the end of their bills.
They are waiting for a movement;
a stirring underneath the silent glass;
a sign to herald the end of their hunger
here, this mizzled Devon morning.

I have watched them in my own stillness
and waited-them-out for what seems like an age,
but they have more patience than I –
they are masters of persistence; models
of how to vanish through your own being.

Once, I watched a flock of blue herons
at Witty's Lagoon, Pacific North West.
Those birds showed the same perseverance;
just as the water there performed
the same tricks it performs here –
in and out, up and down, endlessly circling.

Now the Canada geese have landed,
their elegant vee reduced to a clatter
of ungainly feet across the water's eye
some yards away where the estuary carves
gullies in the slow-emerging silt.
Soon they will begin their long passage
to fly across the Rockies where,
>   even now
my daughter still stands washing her hair
in a turbulent stream eager, perhaps,

to see a grizzly roll from the forest and scoop
a struggling sockeye from the blue.
There is so much potential in her bones
as she flips her wet head back,
slow motion droplets flying in the air.
To her side, her brother slips off
his shirt and shoes, to brave the rushing melt.
He stilts in like a wader; his skin taut. Nascent.

I look up: the herons are gone; the geese too.
It's time to go back home.   I dare not move.

DAFFODILS

There were guards on the bridge spanning the Oder –
one side Slubice, the other East Germany.
They smiled at my mother and called to her
to have a cigarette, pass a little time.
She laughed, gently declined and we walked on
along the bank to where the daffodils grew wild.
My mother let go of my hand so she could pick
and I could run. As I ran I would brush
the swaying blooms with my small palms.
I've never felt so free again.
                                    Back on the bridge
a guard whistled. Beside us the steady river
wound away my mother's cares.
                                    Now every spring
I come to England to work in the fields picking daffodils.
I wear gloves and mostly don't recall
how those bobbing yellow heads blessed my hands.
Mostly I bend and pick, determined and quick,
moving from row to row.
But sometimes I drink and think then
of that border town and the Oder,
quietly unwinding, grey and slow,
the whistling guard,
        the small daffodils of home.

LIGHT ON THE LAKE, ALBERTA

Walking out under a storm-drained sky
we notice a beaver lodge at the water's edge –
a pupil in the eye of the quietened lake.

Pelicans flap across the lens then rise,
their gullets heavy with perch and pickerel.
We scan the flats for signs of hidden life.

The grebes and common loons are searching too,
diving for an evening meal. We alone keep
their company – all the water-sporting families

are back in camp, burning firewood, charring smokies.
A pair of polished eyes emerge – whiskers
flat to face; fur matted to the body.

We lean into our own looking. *There!*
we point in unison, as the creature –
musk rat, otter, beaver, who can tell? –

breaches in the shallows, disappears,
platinum water parting down its flanks.
The stilled surface glows in the animal's absence.
The water gives the clouds back to themselves.

THE LIGHT AT CAPE COD

Motoring out under a yawning Cape sky,
we pass three lighthouses on yellow dunes,
into the oculus of air and ocean.
Shearwaters run upon the sea then rise,
tripping upwards from their light fantastic,
as we scan for humpbacks, minke and fin.

I look around at the whale watchers.
Couples, foreign families, school parties
(the kids all lively, brilliantly cagouled,
their faces airbrushed bright, bouncing in sun),
an old pair, his wispy hair thin as pins,
her skin dulled to flatness with foundation.

Thar she blows! the jubilant kids yell
as a humpback breaches on the starboard
black water sliding like silk down his back.
The fluke print leaves wide emerald circles
as our young guide gabbles in overdrive
and we press the rails for a better look.

The old lady squeezes her husband's hand.
Her bitten fingernails are painted green,
almost the hue of the shivering print.
She smiles up at his liver spotted face
and he shakily bends to kiss her cheek.
The whale slips under the boat and away.

MY RIVER

A river flowed into my township last night.
It wasn't Alice Oswald's Dart, or Wordsworth's Thames,
or Raymond Carver's river that he loved
the way some men love horses or glamorous women.
And it wasn't John Milton's stream at the foot of Paradise
with Satan cloaked in rising mist.
Nor was it T.S. Eliot's river
flowing under the crowds flowing over the bridge,
or Johnson's Fleet Ditch full of unspeakable turds.
It wasn't Carl Sandburg's Desplaines
with its party of happy Hungarians
drinking wine and playing accordions,
or Dylan Thomas's river, in October,
counting off his years towards heaven.
Nor was it Anthony Wilson's river,
down at the mouth of the Exe
with all its sucking *cledge* and *ooze* and *sluice*,
or Auden's *brimming river* singing songs
of love and loss one evening
as it rolled indifferently through the city,
or even Joyce's Liffey running
a way a lone a last a loved a long the...
It was none of these. Neither Neruda's,
nor Shakespeare's with its willows aslant,
nor Keats's with its choir of mourning gnats
borne aloft among the sallows. No...
It was just *a river*. A river
that had run here, seemingly forever,
through the valley, over the mudflats
round the curving oxbow of the harbour
and out of my life.

NOTES

Page 18: MY LAST SEASCAPE

Thomas Luny, maritime painter born in Cornwall 1759. Luny lived in Teignmouth where, despite crippling rheumatism to his hands, he painted some 2,200 paintings until a year or so before his death in 1837.

Page 31: LITHOLOGIES/MYTHLOGIES

Before Smith's map, the date given by Archbishop Ussher – Monday October 23rd 4004 BC – was commonly accepted as the actual date of Earth's creation, and printed at the start of Genesis in the King James Bible.

Page 37: SONG OF A LENGTHMAN

Lengthman: (historical) a rural worker who cleared roadway ditches.

Page 40: THE TIN LODES

Herodotus's Cassiterides – the Tin Islands
Pytheas of Massalia – 3rd century BC, Marseilles
Buddling – prospecting for precious metals with water and sieve
Ictis – St. Michael's Mount
Coffin Works – open cast seams
'What happened to Piran?' – 1919 Levant mine disaster
Bal Maidens – young female mine labourers
Crazing mill – tin ore mill
Tribute – payment for ore
Stopes – the place where ore is cleared
Beelemen – pick-axe handlers
Shambles – broad stairs
Keebles – hoisting buckets
Material Men – mine chandlers and fitters
Tutworker – prospector, miner
Stannum – tin
Winzes – vertical shafts

Page 47: RISE AND FALL: Dagan

Dagan, the fish-god, was an important god of the maritime Canaanites, the Phoenicians.

Page 48: RISE AND FALL: Ceres

In Roman mythology Ceres was a goddess of agriculture, grain crops (she is credited with the invention of spelt wheat), fertility and motherly relationships. She was associated with may (hawthorn) blossom. The young, edible leaves of hawthorn are colloquially known as Bread and Cheese.

Reaper band is taken from the hymn 'Fair waved the Golden Corn' which refers to Canaan's pleasant land. The Canaanites were the forerunners of the Phoenicians who probably visited the British Isles as Roman galley slaves.

Page 57: TRIBUTARIES

For 18 miles between Haytor on Dartmoor and Teignmouth on the south coast, the Templer Way traces the route by which granite was exported from Dartmoor via the Haytor Granite Tramway and the Stover Canal.

Page 58: TRIBUTARIES: The Dark Acre

cleves – cliffs
oggin – the sea
dimmet – dusk
Dewer – the Devil
dinder – thunder
tors – high rocky outcrops
owdry – over cast
ammil – a skin of ice
taw – stream
tawds – toads
toddies – tadpoles
holloway – a sunken lane
brock – badger
unket – dreary
shord – a gap in the hedge
craw – crow
kone – peak of the hedge
mommet – scarecrow
lie-a-biers – the dead
clobb – loam
clats – clods of earth
acker – acre

Acknowledgements

We wish to thank the editors of the following publications, where some of these poems were first published:

Acumen; Atrium; The Beach Hut; The Broadsheet; Caught By The River; The Clearing; Diamond Waterways (Exeter University); *A Fright of Jays* (Maquette, 2015); *The High Window; Haiku Journal; The London Magazine; MAP* (Worple Press, 2014); *Popshot Magazine; Prole Magazine; Stride Magazine; Three Drops From A Cauldron; Driftfish* (Zoomorphic, 2017).

Work from this collaboration was also presented and discussed at the following events, with gratitude to the hosts:

'Vibrant Localism', Exeter University, June 2016;
'Land's End: Imagination, Culture and Society at Coastal Edges', Pendennis Castle, Falmouth, June 2016;
Ways With Words, Dartington Hall, July 2016;
Plymouth Literary Festival, October 2016;
Teignmouth Poetry Festival, March 2017.

'The Tin Lodes' is for Kelvin Corcoran.
'A Sprinkling' is for Eleanor Rees.
'Long Passage' is for Molly and Laurie Shelton.
'Dagan' is for Olivia Woodward.

Indigo Dreams Publishing Ltd
24, Forest Houses
Cookworthy Moor
Halwill
Beaworthy
Devon
EX21 5UU
www.indigodreams.co.uk